The Chapel of St. Anne
Kew Green
1710-1769

Archive material from St.
Anne's Chapel, Kew Green,
transcribed and annotated
by

G. E. CASSIDY

RICHMOND SOCIETY HISTORY SECTION
PAPER No. 2.

1985

ISBN 0 9508198 1 6

Printed by E. H. Baker & Co. Ltd., 86 Lower Mortlake Road, Richmond, Surrey TW9 2JH
Ref. 75242

Foreword

This is the second paper to be published by the History Section of the Richmond Society. The author, George Cassidy, a retired architect living in Kew, and a keen historian of that area, has been concerned for more than 40 years with many aspects of the life of Richmond and Kew. He served for 15 years on the Council of the former Borough of Richmond and was at one time the deputy Mayor. He is a Patron and past Chairman of the Richmond Society, and helped to found its History Section in 1975 acting as Chairman from 1979-1984. During his chairmanship he stimulated his committee to produce a regular journal and an occasional history paper.

George Cassidy has not only been a regular contributor to 'Richmond History' on matters relating to Kew, but has written 'Kew as it Was' for that popular series of photographic records of places in the past. He is also the joint author of a recent book on 'Growing Irises' in a series related to the growing of different plants, and acts as the honorary secretary of the British Iris Society.

Dr. Stephen Pasmore,

Editor, Journal of the
Richmond Society History Section

Introduction

In 1983 I was invited by the Vicar of St. Anne's Church, Kew, to gather together, sort out and advise on the proper disposal of the mass of historical books and documents which had accumulated in the church. This most interesting exercise revealed many documents which shed light on the history of the early years of the Chapel. I felt that it would be of value for these papers to be made more widely available and have therefore put them into order, transcribed many of them and added a few historical notes to maintain some continuity.

The papers cover the period of the establishment of the Chapel from 1710-1714 till 1769 when plans were made for its enlargement to a church by King George III. The papers deal with the founding of the original building and its endowment, and then mainly with the difficulties which arose between the inhabitants and the clergy culminating in the celebrated legal action— *The Attorney General on behalf of the Inhabitants of Kew against Wm. Comer, Clerk, Vicar of Kingston.* A transcription of the Law Report of this case is included.

This booklet is not put forward as a definitive history of Kew Chapel, but as a research document for the benefit of future historians.

I am grateful to the Vicar and Churchwardens of St. Anne's Church for access to the archives and to the History Section of the Richmond Society for arranging this publication.

G. E. Cassidy

ANNE.

Queen Anne

The Chapel of St. Anne, Kew Green
1710-1769

The first roll of subscribers is dated 18th August 1710—

Richard Levett	£21.10	Chris Appleby	£10.15
Sir Chs Eyre	20.00	Thos Howlett	10.00
Leigh Backwell	10.15	Wm. Cox	10.00
John Lely	10.15	Arthur Nixon	10.00
John Murden	10.15	John Martin	5.00
Jos Murden	10.00	Thos Fuller	2.10

Lady Capel added £50. 1st December 1714.

Sir Richard Levett lived in the Dairie House. This was part of the estate of Sir Wm Brownlow, previously owned by the Ancrans and the Portmans, Sir Richard took over the lease from Sir John Portman in 1697 and purchased the property from Sir Wm Brownlow in 1703. He died 31st January 1710/11.

Sir Charles Eyre was one time Governor of Bengal. He had the lease of one of the houses between the Dutch House (Dairie House) and the Ferry, later leased by Queen Caroline, and known as the Queen's House. He died in 1729.

Leigh Backwell had the other house between the Dutch House and the ferry, known as Ferry House.

John Lely was the grandson of Sir Peter Lely, the painter. He lived in the house west of Hanover House.

John Murden and Jos Murden had property on the North side of Kew Green. John Murden and Thos Fuller afterwards refused to pay their subscriptions and on the 29th May 1716 a declaration was signed and sealed by the other subscribers which appointed John Gaine of Kew Green to ask, demand and receive the subscriptions and, in default, to exhibit a Bill in the Court of Chancery.

Christopher Appleby was the eldest son and heir of Lancelot Appleby of Brinzey, Somerset. He was admitted to the Middle Temple, 7th May, 1694, but was not called to the Bar. He had Chambers in the Middle Temple but lived at Kew. It is possible that in 1710 he was renting part of the property on the south side of Kew Green which included Cambridge Cottage and Church House then owned by Richard Mounteney and his wife, Anne. He purchased this property later (741—747 in the 1771 survey).

In 1717 Appleby was named as a trustee for Anne Mounteney.

As a lawyer he was clearly legal adviser to the village and looked after the affairs of the Chapel until his death in 1744.

Thos Howlett lived on the east side of Kew Green. He died in 1759.

Wm Cox and probably Thos Fuller lived on the east side of Kew Green.

Arthur Nixon lived on the south side of Kew Green.

With this financial support the inhabitants petitioned the Queen, as Lady of the Manor of Richmond, of which Kew was part, for permission to erect a Chapel at Kew as a Chapel of Ease in the Parish of Kingston on Thames.

The petition was supported by the Vicar of Kingston, the Revd. Gideon Harding, who wrote in the margin:

"The Hamlet of Kew, being within my parish of Kingston, I do most heartily concur, and as far as my right is concerned, do hereby consent to so much of the prayer of this petition as relates to a building of a Chapple there"

The Queen gave her consent and the following Warrant was issued: —
Anne R.

ANNE by the Grace of God Queen of Great Britain France and Ireland Defender of the Faith etc. To all to whom these presents shall come GREETING WHEREAS many of our Good subjects inhabitants of the Hamlet of Kew within the parish of Kingston upon Thames in our County of Surrey have by their petition humbly represented unto Us that by reason of their very great distance from their said Parish Church and from any the Chappells of Ease belonging thereunto Whereof Richmond, which is a mile distant is the nearest to them, they are hindered from resorting so frequently as they ought to the publique worship of God which they esteem a most greivous calamity and have therefore most humbly prayed inasmuch as they have begun and by the blessing of God on their endeavours with great success carried on a subscription for erecting a Chappel and have obtained the consent of the present Vicar of Kingston for that purpose to which parish the said Chappell when erected is meant to be another Chappell of Ease, that We would be graciously pleased to Grant them Our leave (the said Hamlet of Kew being part of Our mannor of Richmond) to erect and build the said Chappell on the south side of Kew Green on an antient Gravell Pit or peice of wast ground adjoyning to the Road there at this time of no use or advantage to Us or the said Inhabitants but very convenient for this purpose To which request Wee as well from a due consideracon had of a Report layd before Us which was made to Our High Treasurer by Our Attorney Generall on the said Peticon as out of Our Princely Zeal to promote and encourage the pious and good intencons of Our Loving Subjects are Gratiously pleased to condescend and agree KNOW YEE THEREFORE That Wee have given and granted and by these presents do give and grant unto the said Inhabitants of the Hamlet of Kew now and for the time being or such person or persons as is are or shall be nominated or appointed by them in this behalfe free liberty leave lycence and authority to erect and build or cause to be erected and built on the said Gravell Pit or any part thereof (being the wast ground within Our said Mannor of Richmond) a Chappel to be used by them in all times coming for celebrating Divine Worship according to the Liturgy and usage of the Church of England And Wee do also give full power leave

8

liberty lycence and authority unto the said Inhabitants now and for the time being or such person or persons as is are or shall be nominated and appointed by them in this behalfe to enclose with a wall or otherwise as to them shall seem meet so much ground whereon to erect and build the said Chappell and for encompassing thereof, as by admeasurement shall amount to One Hundred foot square, which said Chappell is to be erected and built and the said Enclosure made at the charge of the said Inhabitants and by and out of the moneys raised or to be raised by the said subscripcon and to be deemed and taken when built as another Chappel of Ease to the Parish Church of our said Towne of Kingston upon Thames as aforesaid And moreover Wee do hereby will and require all Our Officers Ministers and Loving Subjects whatsoever whom this may concerne to permit and suffer Our said Inhabitants now and for the time being or such person or persons as is are or shall be appointed by them in this behalfe to begin carry on and finish the said Building for a Chappel and the Enclosure for encompassing thereof in manner aforesaid without any let hindrance or molestacon whatsoever as they will answer the contrary at their perills And this being first entred in the Rolls or Court Books of Our Mannor of Richmond And in the Office of the Auditor of Our Land Revenues arising within Our County of Surrey shall be not only to our said Inhabitants but to all others that shall or may be concerned herein a sufficient warrant. GIVEN at Our Court at Kensington the 28th day of June 1712 In the Eleventh Year of Our Reigne.

By Her Maj. Command

OXFORD

The inhabitants moved swiftly in the matter and on the 30th June 1712 the following Agreement was signed: —

> Wee whose names are hereunto subscribed Inhabitants of the Hamlet of Kew within the parrish of Kingston upon Thames in the County of Surry and Subscribers for erecting a Chapple of ease to our sd parrish church, in & upon Kew Green within our Hamlet aforesaid and for that purpose having obtayned her Majestys most Gracious Licence under her Royal signed Manual impowering us or the Major part of us to erect & build the sd Chapple Have in order to the effectual carrying on and finishing thereof come to following agreements & resolucons in relacon thereto

Impris Wee doo agree & resolve that all such sum or sums of money as have been or shall be subscribed for erecting or finishing the sd Chapple shall be forthwith paid unto Sir Charles Eyre Kt (he having been pleased to take the trouble upon him of receiving and paying the sd money) and that he the sd Sir Chas Eyre shall give to each subscriber a receipt for the money he receives promising to repay the same if the sd intended building shall not be begun ?before Michas day next.

9

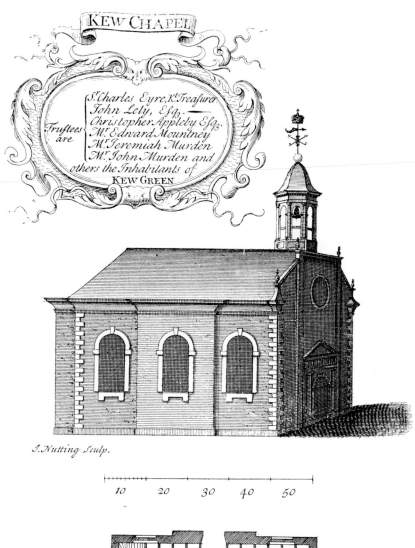

J. Nutting Sculp.

10   20   30   40   50

Recordare eorum Deus mi, in hâc re, et ne finito deleri benignitates
quas exercuerunt erga Domum Dei et erga observationes ejus.

Kew Chapel. The frontispiece to the published charity sermon preached by Lewis
Stephens on 12 May, 1721. (By courtesy of the Richmond Library).

Item. That the sd Sir Charles Eyre John Lely Esq Christopher Appleby Jeremiah Murden John Murden Arthur Nixon Wm Cox Thomas Howlet or any three of them (of which Sir Charles Eyre John Lely or Christopher Appleby to be one) shall be trustees for erecting & building the sd Chapple and for making contracts with workmen buying materials directing the payment of money and dooing all other matters in relacon to the sd building and what they or any three of them as aforesaid shall do is to be binding & conclusive for all the subscribers

Item. That the sd persons or any three of them of which the sd John Lely or Christopher Appleby to be one before any money is paid by Sir Charles Eyre shall signe the workmans bill or a direccon or authority to the sd Sir Charles Eyre to pay the sd money and the workmans or other persons receipt under that direccon shall be a good discharge unto the sd Sir Charles Eyre for what he shall pay.

Item. That the intended Chapple shall not exceed 60 feet in length 27 feet in breath and the walls thereof 18 feet in height from the surface of the Ground and that the Chancell shall not exceed tenn feet in length and that there shall be four windows in the south front of the sd Chapple and a door in the midst of that front one window in the Chancell 5 windows in the North front a door in ye west end and a window over it and that ye sd Chapple shall be erected in the place menconed in Her Majestys Royal signed Manuall and when the sum of £250: shall be received by the sd Sir Charles Eyre the sd Chapple shall begin to be built. Lastly that the trustees or any 3 of them as aforesaid shall from time to time as they see occacon summon all the subscribers to meet in order to the making of such trust or agreement or resolcon as shall be necessary to compleat & carry on the sd building and that there shall be kept a publick book wherein shall be entered all ye proceedings which hitherto have or at any time hereafter shall be carryed on in relacon to ye sd Chapple such book shall remain in the hands of the sd Sir Charles Eyre to be from time to time inspected by such of the subscribers who shall request or desire to see the same.

Dated this 30th June 1712.

Arthur Nixon
Thos Howlett
Margarett Harris
Edward Lyford
Tho Powell his mark
Michaell Layton
The mark of Tho Fuller
Chris Appleby
    1712

Charles Eyre
Jno Lely
Ann Mounteney

(Ann Mounteney, wife of Richard Mounteney, Margarett Harris, Edward Lyford, Thos Powell and Michael Layton were additional subscribers to the first list)

In their petition to the Queen the inhabitants had asked for 80 oaks out of the new Park and Lord Oxford calling for a report, Edward Wilcox reported as follows:—

(A coppy
The original with Mr
Tilson in ye Treasury)

To the most honble Robert Earl of Oxford and Earl Mortimer Ld High Treasurer of Great Brittain

The Inhabitants of the Hamlet of Kew within the Parrish of Kingston upon Thames & within Her Majestys Mannor of Richmond in ye County of Surry which is at least three miles distant from their parrish Church having by their humble peticon obteyned her Majestys Royal signed Manual impowering them to erect a Chapple on some part of the Wast Ground within the sd Hamlett for celebrating divine worship according to the litturgy & usage of the Church of England and having also by the same peticon humbly prayed that Her Majesty would be gratiously pleased to grant them 80 oaks out of new Park towards building wainscotting & pewing the sd Chapple which your Lordship was pleased to direct me to consider and report to your Lordship my opinion thereupon.

In obedience thereto I humbly represent to your Lordship that the sd park is not very well stocked with Timber Trees fitt for such service and in regard a considerable quantity of trees have been felled these three years which have generally fallen decayed at ye bottom and more must be next year to be used about & pay for repairs I am humbly of opinion so Great a number of Good Timber Trees as is desired cannot conveniently be spared out of the sd park. And having discoursed the agent for the petrs in order to reduce the number of Trees peticoned for he does assure me that notwithstanding utmost indeavours have been used to get subscriptions for building the sd Chappel yet such subscriptions fall short £100 & upwards of what the same will cost. That the petrs have begun the sd work and built the walls thereof at least five feet within the ground in hopes of Her Maiestys further Bounty towards carrying on so good a work without which they shall not be able to effect the same or reap the benefit intended them & their Posterity by Her Majestys Royal Sign Manuall hereinbefore menconed. And tho I cannot but say there may be as many trees felled in ye sd park as may be worth £100 yet the felling thereof and even those for repair of the Earl of Rochesters rooms I dislike fearing it may deface the Park.

If her Maiesty shall be gratiously pleased to bestow anything on them toward perfecting the said work either in trees or in other ways as your Lordship shall think most convenient. The direction of the same is most humbly submitted.

to your Lordships Great Wisdom

27 Decr 1712.   Edw Wilcox

12

The inhabitants had already (20th March 1712) drafted some suggested ways of raising the money they required: —

> If it be inconvient to her Majesty to bestow her Royall Benefacon to the Inhabitants of Kew in money Their humble request may be answered by either of these three wayes.

> First altho not by Timber Trees yett by moneys ariseing by sale of wood felled or to be felled in new Park.

> 2. By Timber Trees or money to be raised by sale of Timber and Wood by Mr. Wilcocks the Surveyor out of other woods or forests whereof he is Surveyor he having a Warrant for his indemnity.

> 3. By directing a warrant to General Cholmley Steward of the Mannor of Richmond forthwith to Levy the arrears of all the Demesne Rents Quitt Rents and other Rents of that Mannor and thereout to pay Sir Charles Eyre Knight in trust for the Inhabitants of Kew towards the building of the Chappell there such sums as her Majesty shall please.

It seems likely that this was a draft prepared by Christopher Appleby and that he was the agent whom Wilcox met and that he had a hand in preparing the following petition submitted to Lord Oxford: —

> To the most Honble Robert Earl of Oxford & Earl Mortimer Ld. High Treasurer of Great Britain.

> The humble petition and Memorial of the Inhabitants of Kew within the Parrish of Kingston upon Thames many of which are Her Majestys tennants within her mannor of Richmond in Surry.

> Most Humbly Sheweth

> That the said inhabitants having obteynded her Majestys Royal Licence & authority under her signe manual to erect a Chapel of ease to their said Parrish Church on Kew Green for the Worship & service of Almighty God according to the litturgy of the Church of England and towards the building thereof the said Inhabitants and other pious and well disposed Benefactors having voluntarily subscribed severall summs of money but such subscriptions not being sufficient to compleat the said building your petrs by their petition to her Majesty prayed her to bestow upon them as of her Royal Bounty 80 Oaks out of Richmond Park the consideration of which your Lordship referred to Edw Wilcox Esq her Maiestys Surveyor who has made his report in obedience thereto which is hereto annexed By which Report he is of opinion that so great a quantity of Good Timber Trees cannot conveniently spared out of the Park but that your petrs having begun the work in hope of her Maiestys further Bounty cannot without the same effect such work or reap the benefit intended them and their posterity by her Majestys said Royal signe Manual and though he cannot but say there may as many trees be felled out of that Park as may be worth £100 (being the summ wanted to compleat the building) yet the Earl of Rochester seems to dislike the

felling thereof fearing it may deface the Park and if her Majesty shall be gratiously pleased to bestow anything on your petrs towards perfecting this work in Trees or otherwise the direction of the same is by such Report most humbly submitted to your Lordshipps wisdom.

That your petrs having begun to build the sd Chapple and finding their subscriptions not sufficient to finish the same by the summ of £100, most humbly hope they shall be partakers of her Majestys Royal contribution and bounty to enable them to compleat the same.

And therefore if your Lordshipp upon reading the sd Mr. Wilcox's report shall be of opinion that it is not convenient to grant your petrs any trees out of Richmond Park they most humbly pray your Lordshipp to referr it back to the said Mr. Wilcox to certify whether such number of Trees as your Lordshipp shall think proper or some certeyn pecuniary benefaction instead thereof may not with more conveniency be granted or raised for your petrs out of some other of her Majestys Parks or Forests whereof he is Surveyor or that your Lordshipp will be pleased to make such other order upon the sd Report to enable your petrs to compleat the sd building and thereby reap the benefit intended for them and their posterity by her Sacred Majestys signe Manual aforesaid as in your Lordshipps great wisdom & goodness shall seem most proper

And your petrs shall ever pray etc.

There is a note on this document "18th Mar 1712/13. My Lord to have a copy & he will move the Queen thereupon"

This he did with some success and the following Warrant was issued: —

Anne R.

Our will and pleasure is that by virtue of our Generall Letters of Privy Seal bearing date the 13th day of March 1701 you issue and pay or cause to be issued and paid unto the Inhabitants of the Hamlet of Kew within the Parish of Kingston upon Thames in our County of Surrey or such person or persons as is are or shall be nominated and appointed by them in this behalfe the sum of One Hundred Pounds without Acco: Wee being gratiously pleased to assist the said Inhabitants with that sum as a Voluntary Conribucon from Us towards the Charge of Compleating the Chappell which they by subscripcon and Our permission have begun to erect and build on a piece of Wast Ground within our Mannor of Richmond to be used by them in all times coming for Celebrating Divine Worship according to the Liturgy and usage of ye Church of England And Our Further Pleasure is that you cause the said sum of £100 for ye purpose aforesaid to be satisfyed by Levying Tallys on ye Bailliff or Collector of ye Rents Issues and Profitts of our said Mannor of Richmond or on ye Receiver of Our Land Revenues within our said County of Surrey both or either of them as the said inhabitants or such as are or shall be appointed by them to receive the same shall in that case desire And for so doing this shall be your Warrant Given at Our Court at Windsor Castle the 14th Day of October

1713 in ye 12th year of Our Reign
By her Maj Command,
Oxford.

To Our Right Trusty and Rt. Welbeloved
Cousin and Councel Robt. Earl of Oxford
& Earl of Mortimer—
High Treasurer of Great Britain.

Lord Oxford sent to Lord Halifax—Auditor of Receipt for Her Majestys Exchequer—an order to pay the sum of £100—dated 27th Oct 1713 This sum was received by Christopher Appleby on the 19th Nov 1713.

The work on the Chapel proceeded with Mr. Martin as carpenter and Mr. Robinson as bricklayer.

Christopher Appleby wrote in 1715, when appealing to the Governors of Queen Anne's Bounty,

Her Majesty, as she passed the Road to her Pallace at Windsor, allways stopped her coach, whilst it was building and when it was finished at a place where it could be seen, and used to call it 'Her Little Church'

but the Bishop of Winchester refused to grant a License for the Consecration without some assurance that the Chapel was sufficiently endowed to provide for the repair of the building and for the curate's stipend. More funds were urgently equired and by good fortune were available. £50 was provided by Dr. Slare out of the estate of Samuel Neale and was received by Christopher Appleby on the 16th April 1714.

To this sum was added £30 by the inhabitants and for the £80, Sir Charles Eyre, John Lely and Christopher Appleby, by deed dated 16th April 1714, purchased the lease of certain woods and wood grounds known henceforth as the 'Woodlands'. These comprised three woods in the parishes of Assingdon, Hawkwell alias Hockley and South Fambridge in the County of Essex, known as Witthorp Wood of 8 acres, 18 acre wood of 18 acres and Shoulder of Mutton Wood of 12 acres. On the 17th April 1714 these woods were assigned to one Jonathan Fogg, Gent of London, to hold in trust for the residue of 500 years on behalf of the inhabitants of Kew 'to apply the proceeds in the first instance to keep the Chapel in repair and to apply the surplus, if any, and the whole until such repair should be wanted, towards the maintenance of the Curate of the Chapel'. The income from the Woodlands at that time was £4-5. per annum.

The Bishop accepted this endowment as satisfactory but in consequence of its smallness himself gave 20 guineas and the offerings at the Consecration upon the promise that the endowment would be augmented as speedily as possible.

The Chapel was consecrated on the 12th May 1714 and dedicated to St. Anne. The sermon was preached by the Vicar of Kingston, the Revd.

15

Of the Houſe of Prayer.

A
SERMON

Preach'd at the

CONSECRATION

OF THE

CHAPEL at *KEW*,

Within the PARISH of

KINGSTON on THAMES,

- On *Wedneſday, May* 12. 1714,

Before the RIGHT REVEREND Father in God

JONATHAN Lord Biſhop of WINTON.

By JOHN BROUGHTON, Vicar of the Mother Church at *King-ſton* on *Thames.*

Publiſh'd at the Deſire of the Gentlemen, and others, that heard it.

LONDON:
Printed by *W. B.* for R. SARE near *Grays-Inn* Gate, and
E. PLACE at *Furnivalls-Inn* Gate in *Holborn,* 1714.

John Boughton, D.D. who appointed as the first curate, the Revd. Thomas Fogg.

The cost of building the Chapel was £500 which was said to be double the amount estimated. Lady Capel gave a further £50 but a considerable sum, approximately £150, had still to be found. On the 22nd April 1715 the inhabitants agreed to pay this off by an annual rate of 1/- in the pound on the value of their properties. A detailed schedule was drawn up and signed which showed that in the years 1714-1718 the amount so promised was £130.15.2d. This scheme did not take complete effect and by 1718 some £50 was still outstanding and this was obtained on a bond at interest and the workmen finally paid off.

At a meeting on the 27th July 1719 a number of the subscribers agreed to pay the following sums to extinguish the bond:—

The Rt. Hon. Lady Capell	Five pounds
Charles Eyre	Seven pounds
John Lely	Five pounds
Chris Appleby	Five pounds
John Broun	Tenn pounds
S. Mollyneux	Five pounds

The promise to the Bishop to augment the endowment was next fulfilled. Under the settlement of Dr. Slare's Charity out of the Neale estate, by decree of the Court of Chancery, a further £150 was paid to the inhabitants. This sum, together with gifts from John Lely and others of £33.10s and Christopher Appleby of £2.10s, was invested in the Queen's Lottery of 1713, course 15, and with interest and part of the collections at the Chapel realised some £220. This was paid to the Governors of Queen Anne's Bounty who, in 1716, added a further £200. for the endowment of the Chapel.

So the First Augmentation was the purchase, in Nov. 1716, for £360 of the lands known as Pulpits Farm in Essex, adjoining the 'Woodlands' for the endowment of the curacy. Pulpits Farm was described in the records of the Bounty Office as follows:—

'All that Messuage, Tenements or Farm with the appurtenances called or known by the name of Pokepetts Tenements alias Pokepetts and the Lands, Tenements and Heriditaments thereunto belonging called or known by the several names, herein after-mentioned (that is to say) Three Crofts thereof known by the name of Broomehill heretofore called Beldeland alias Belland containing by estimation Eighteen Acres be the same more or less, three other crofts or parcels of land called Hangdmenshot containing by estimation Eighteen Acres, be the same more or less, one parcel of Meadow, containing by estimation Two Acres, be the same more or less, called Pokepetts Mead, Two crofts of land called Perrymans Croft alias Perryfields, containing by estimation eight acres, be the same more or less, one other Croft called Nutt Croft, containing by estimation Six Acres, be the same more or less—Four Crofts or parcels of land anciently called Woodfield & since Woodland,

17

containing by estimation Eighteen Acres be the same more or less,—and four Closes or parcels of land called Peverells alias Peverly Space, Lees Home Croft and Sheer Croft, or by whatsoever name or names the same or any of them, are or have been called or known and all the Orchards, Gardens, Backsides, Outhouses, Buildings & Appurtenances, Lands, Tenements, Woods, Underwoods, Commodities, Hereditaments, & Appurtenances thereunto belonging or in any wise appertaining or therewith, now or at any time heretofore had, held, used or occupied or enjoyed or accepted, reputed, taken or known, as Part Parcel or Member thereof or appurtenant thereto, situate, lying or being in the Towns, Parishes & Fields of South Fambridge, Ashindon alias Ashendon & Hackwell, alias Hawkswell or any of them of the same County.'

(Note: These lands of 70 acres more or less produced an income of about £20. In the Terrier of 1771, Pulpits Farm was described as being of 60 acres or thereabouts, let on a lease of 21 years from Michaelmas 1770 to Martin Lurring at the yearly rent of £25. In 1801 the lands were declared by the tenant as being of 53 acres and the annual rent was £30. In 1802 the lands were surveyed by George Basset, Land Surveyor, as 56 acres. In 1805 the rent was increased to £66. per annum and in 1811 the rent was increased by the amount of Land Tax redeemed, £2.8s.)

Thomas Fogg, as soon as he was appointed curate, because of the smallness of the endowment, arranged with the inhabitants that they would pay him the rentals of the pews they occupied which totalled £72. He soon had a disagreement with Mr. Appleby about the disposal of the Sacrament money and offended him by referring the matter personally to the Bishop. He wrote to Mr. Appleby on the 10th July 1715:

Sir,

I own I could not but be surprised at ye grand estrangement which I observed in Mr. Appleby towards me, and as much was I pushed to guess ye reason, till discoursing lately with Sir Charles I found it was my speaking to ye Bishop in relation to ye distribution of ye moneys collected at ye Sacrament.

For my own part, I was ready to lay hold of ye first opportunity that offer'd itself, of having his Lordship's determination of ye case, and thought Mr. Lely being present, none could be more proper than that I made use of. I presume he may have informed you, ye displeasure ye Bishop was pleased to express against any other application of ye Collections than that I insisted on long since, it being according to ye order of ye Church and therefore I am obliged in Duty to know no other.

However, Sir Charles acquainting me with your uneasiness on ye head I have not, as yet, disposed of any of ye money collected, except that on Easter Day, which by His Lordship's express order I have taken entirely to my self. If therefore you shall think fit to wait upon ye Bishop to know his further pleasure—It shall be punctually observed as soon as known. Otherwise I must conform to what he has already enjoyn'd me.

I desire ye favour of an answer, and hoping nothing will be ever able to create ye least misunderstanding between a Person from whom I have received such accumulated favours, and my self,

am

Sir,

Your most oblig'd

humble servant

Thos Fogg.

Kew. July ye 10th 1715.

On July 26th, Sir Charles Eyre sought to pour oil on troubled waters and wrote to Mr. Appleby:—

Sir,

I am sorry for Mr. Foggs indiscretion in having offered or said anything disrespectfull or reflecting on you for I'm sure you have been the best of friends to him and the first promoter of anything that he can lay claim to and therefore let me begg of you to pass by any Indiscreet word for tho he be an Ingenious young fellow he wants years over his head and you know youth is hott but upon recollection brought to better temper. If you could have stayed to have attended that affair yesterday morning it would have been determined by the Bishop in the presence of us three, though you and I without Mr. Fogg can at any time know the Bishop's pleasure which he may signifie under his hand to Mr Fogg and in my opinion will doe better—and be more effectuall to the first design than if Mr Fogg were present at the determination.

I hope you wont think of laying aside any future pains or care that may Contribute to the good of the Chappel for you know 'tis God's work and he has bless'd our Endeavours hitherto and don't let us be wanting to ourselves for the behaviour or inconsiderate Expressions of the Priest. I shall say nothing to that part of your letter of withdrawing subscription because I know you are a man of more honour and integrity. Herewith comes a Baskett of the Ripest Morella Cherrys which dispose of as you think fitt with my humble service to Mr Anonymous, your good Lady & Second and Accept the same from

sir

Your Obedt & humble Servt

Charles Eyre.

Tuesday Night
July 26th 1715
Pray return the Baskett
by Layton for I vallue it
much.

In his determination of this matter the Bishop commanded that the Sacrament Money should be disposed of as follows:

The Collection on Easter Day was to be entirely the Ministers; the other

19

collections to be disposed of at the Discretion of him and the Chapple Warden.

Sir Charles Eyre, then Chapplewarden, was all for converting the whole collection to the Chapple, at length being Nov 6th 1715 the Minister and Sir Charles did agree that considering that there were not many poor on the place that the Priest, from the Sentences appointed to be read at the Offertory as well as from the practice of the Primitive Church, had a rt. to share in the collection and further that there was not a rate suffict for defraying the necessary charges relating to the Chapple, That upon their several accounts the moneys collected at the Sacrament shod be divided into three equal portions, the one the Ministers, the second the Chappell the 3rd the poor (excepting that on Easter Day)

Mr Fogg claimed that he had complied with this command and agreement but the inhabitants were divided in opinion. His supporters testified on his behalf: —

These are to Certify whom it may concern that the Revd. Mr Thos Fogg Minister of St. Anne Kew Chapple in the County of Surrey has behaved himself the space of three years which is the time since the Consecration hereof in all parts of his ministeriall Function with Piety and Devotion.

That he is of a Sober Life and Conversation & well affected to the present Establishment in Church & State. In Witness whereof wee the Inabitants of the Hamlett of Kew have set our hands this 15th May 1717.

D. Capell   Percivall

Jo Gaine

Hen Gaine

John Lely

Hen Harrington

Nat Mounteney

Jo Murden

Jo Schute

Arth Nixon

There were other grounds for complain against Mr Fogg and the following petition was probably instigated by Mr Appleby and sent to the Bishop.

To the Right Reverend Father in God Jonathan Ld Bishop of Winton.

The Humble Representation of the Inhabitants of Kew Green in the County of Surrey whose Names are hereto in behalf of them & the rest of the Inhabitants

Most Humbly Sheweth

That the said Inhabitants and Severall other well disposed persons Assisted by her late most Sacred Majesty Queen Anne by voluntary Subscriptions Erected and built a Chappel on Kew Green for the Worshipp and Service of Almighty God according to the Littergy & Service of the Church of England which has been consecrated by your Lordshipp and Endowed with Lands of Inheritance to the Annuall Value of £25 & upwards and your petrs and others by Voluntary yearly payments for their pews have increased the yearly revenues of the said Chappell unto the sum of £100 a year or thereabouts and your Lordshipp was pleased to Licence the Reverend Mr Thomas Fogg to be the Curate of the said Chappell.

That after the said Inhabitants had Cheerfully Expended very great sumes of money in the building Endowment and increasing the Revenues of the said Chappell they had reason to hope and expect that the said Curate having so great encouragement as aforesaid would have constantly resided at Kew Green that he might have been Always ready to have performed the Severall parts and Offices of his Ministeriall function especially in case of necessity as the Administration of Baptism to Infants in danger of Death in instructing youth in the Principalls of the Christian Religion and Church Cattechism and in praying with sick persons and Administering the blessed Sacrament to them in the latest of extremity in case of any sudden and dangerous Illness and that every one of the said inhabitants from the richest to the poorest as their severall cases required should have been partakers of all such Comforts and blessings as might be Justly Expected where such Curate duly Discharges the Duty of his Ministry and in return receives the hearty Affection and Love of those comitted to his care as well as their money.

But 'tis with the utmost concern and uneasyness that the said inhabitants find themselves totally disappointed in such their just Expectacons and that 'tis their duty to represent to your Lordshipp the severall matters of fact contained in the following Articles.

1st.

That the said Mr Thomas Fogg does not think fitt to live at or near to Kew Green by reason whereof the said Inhabitants in cases of necessity are destitute of Assistance from him and have severall times been Obleidged if they could to get some other minister to Officiate in his room and when they have not been able so to doe Severall great inconveniences have happened and many more may hereafter happen and especially with respect to the particulars before menconed.

The said Inhabitants doe admitt that Mr Tho Fogg (to give some colour to a pretended residence) has taken lodgings on Kew Green by the year but it so far from using the same for the constant place of his habitation that he seldom or never lyes there but on Saturday Nights and at other times on Weekdays does not use the said Lodging so much as to exchange his Riding Clothes for his Cannonical habitt itt being the constant practice of the said Mr Thos Fogg such Weekdays and hollydays as he pleases to officiate in the said Chappel to read the Divine Service in his Boots and Riding Clothes under the Surplice without giving himselfe the trouble and uneasyness of Exchanging the same for his Gown and Cassock so that he may with more expedition retire from the

Chapple when the service is over to the place of his reall residence which is either at his fathers house in Mark Lane London or at his Brothers on Hounslow Heath.

2nd.

The said Thomas Fogg hath never obeyed your Lordshipps particular direction as to the ringing and Tolling of the Bell which instead of half and hour is never permitted to ring and toll in all above 10 or 15 minutes at the most such is the great hast of him the said Thomas Fogg to get over the Service that he may leave his Cure and Such Speed used in beginning of the same which allways putts a stop to the Ringing of the Bell that many times it is not permitted to Toll above 3 or 4 minutes and tho several of the Inhabitants are using their utmost care and Speed to get into the Chappell before the Service begins and are in Sight of the same yet such extreme hast is used in reading that the said Curate gets into the first Lesson or the Psalmes and most commonly beyond the confession and Absolution before 'tis possible for the Inhabitants to get into the Chappell, all which would be Effectually prevented if the Said Mr Fogg thought fitt to obey your Lordshipps Commands and permit the bell to ring one Quarter and then to Toll another Quarter of an hour:

3rd.

The said Thomas Fogg Seldom or never Catechises the children Nor ever reads the most Excellt Exhortacon to the Communion the Sunday before the intended celebration contenting himselfe with giving the Inhabitants notice thereof in these or the like words: The Holy Sacrament will be here Administered on Sunday Next.

4th.

The said Thomas Fogg often times permitts the Divine Service of the Church to be Omitted and Unperformed on Wednesdays and Fridays Especially if there happens any hollydays in the same week and Usually hires such persons to read the prayers for him as are not in Preists Orders, Whereby the Inhabitants when such Deacon officiates are deprived of the benefitt of Absolution and when the said Mr Fogg Officiates himselfe he reads the Service with so low a voice that he cannot be heard but only by a very few of the Inhabitants who are seated near him.

5th.

The said Thomas Fogg insists to keep and detaine for his own private use and occasion (for anything wee know to the contrary) All the money collected at the Sacrament and altho often desired utterly refuse to distribute the same for the reliefe of the poor inhabitants or to let them know to what pious or Charitable uses the same is applyed and altho the said inhabitants have dilligently inquired they are not able to discover that he hath given away any of the said money or at least but a very small and inconsiderable part thereof to any of the poor inhabitants within his said Curacy:

All which matters are in all humillity represented unto your Lordshipp by the said Inhabitants who humbly request your Lordshipp to recall the Lycence you have been pleased to grant unto the said Mr Tho Fogg and to discharge him from further officiating in the said Chappell OR at least that your Lordshipp will please to Obleidge him constantly to live inhabitt and really reside at Kew Green and to give the Inhabitants such relief in the matters hereby represented as may tend to the glory of God the good and peace of the Church and to the Establishing a good Agreement for the future between the said Mr Fogg and those who shall live under his Cure.

John Murden Chappell Warden
Chris Appleby 1717

Charles Eyre
Jno Lely
John Gaine
Arthur Nixon
John Martyn
William Cox
Thos Howlett
John Hayter

The Bishop did not recall the licence but isued the following order:

Jonathan by divine permission Bishop of Winton to all whom these presents may concern Greeting WHEREAS we have received a paper entituled The Humble Representation of the Inhabitants of Kew Green in the County of Surrey & conteining several Articles of Complaint against Mr Thomas Fogg Curate of St Anne Kew Chappel and subscribed by Sir Charles Eyre Knight Christopher Appleby John Murden and others of the said inhabitants AND WHEREAS we have likewise received from the said Mr Fogg a paper entituled An Answer to the representation of Sir Charles Eyre Mr Appleby and others WEE after mature deliberation upon the premisses & out of our tender regard for the spiritual good and wellfare of the inhabitants aforesaid have thought fit to make the following Orders:

First Wee require and enjoin Mr Thomas Fogg Curate of St. Anne Kew Chappel in the County of Surrey and our diocese of Winton to reside duly and regularly upon his said Cure by living or lodging in some house at Kew Green or within the Hamlett of Kew

Secondly we order and require that all moneys collected at the sacrament be disposed of for the future to pious and charitable uses and in such manner as the Rubrick at the end of the communion service in the book of common prayer in that case directs

Thirdly and WHEREAS the inhabitants of Kew Green aforesaid in their said representation doe set forth that Mr Fogg hath been remiss and negligent in catechiseing the children WEE order and require him the said Mr Fogg to examine and instruct the children of the inhabitants publickly in the Chappel in the Catechism of the Church of England and at least every Sunday during the time of Lent and that instead of a sermon in the Afternoon he doe expound upon some part of the said catechism

Lastly WEE enjoin the said Mr Fogg to read Morning Prayer in the Chappel aforesaid every holyday and every Wednesday and Fryday throughout the year and that the inhabitants may have due notice of the time of prayer Wee require the Bell belonging to the said Chappel to be run a quarter of an hour at least and to be tolled another quarter before the beginning of Divine Service and if at any time hereafter the said Mr Fogg shall be hinder'd by sickness or called by his lawful occasions from his personal attendance on the duties of his ministerial Function Wee will and require him to provide and appoint as his Deputy or Assistant a person who is in the Order of Priesthood and who for his learning and goodly Conversation is duly qualified for the discharge of so weighty a Trust GIVEN under our Episcopal Seale dated the fifteenth of February in the year of our Lord 1717 English Style and of our consecration the eleventh.

JONAT WINCHESTER

There appears to have been no further trouble with Mr Fogg and his stipend was increased to £100 per annum. He was succeeded as Curate by the Revd Mr Hill but there is no record of the date of this change. From 1726 to about 1733 the Revd Hugh was at least a part time Curate and attended meetings of the vestry.

Changes were taking place. In 1728 John Lely died and in 1729 Sir Charles Eyre also died, leaving Christopher Appleby as the survivor of the real founders of the Chapel. He had been active in the augmentation of the endowment. He was executor of the estate of Dame Elizabeth Holford, of the Parish of All Hallows in the City of London, who left £200 to Queen Anne's Bounty for the endowment of St Anne's. In 1724 the Governors of the Bounty added a further £200—all invested at 4% per annum. In 1721 the death occurred of the Hon. Dorothy Lady Capell, Dowager Baroness of Tewkesbury who had lived in Kew House. She left £10 per annum to be charged to her estate for the benefit of the Chapel provided her heirs should ever enjoy her two pews and the vault she had built. She also left Perry Court Farm with 150 acres in the parishes of Preston, Ludenham, Ospringe and Faversham in the County of Kent, then in the possession of Mr. William Symonds and about the yearly value of £105 in trust in the following terms : —

NOW my Will and mind is, AND I do hereby give, devise and bequeath all that my said Farm and Lands called Perry alias Perry Court with the closes and thereto belonging and all other my Lands Tenements and Heriditaments in the said County of Kent, and the Reversion and Reversions Remainder and Remainders Rents Issues and Profits thereof and of every part thereof unto the Hon Samuel Molyneux Esq principal Secretary to his Royal Highness George Prince of Wales, Sir Philip

24

Jackson of Richmond in the County of Surrey Kt. John Lely of Kew Green aforesaid Esq and Christopher Appleby of The Middle Temple London Gent and their heirs TO HAVE AND TO HOLD unto them UPON TRUST that they shall immediately upon and after my decease enter upon the said premises in the said County of Kent and receive and take the Rents Issues and Profits thereof from the Feast of the Annunciation of the Blessed Virgin Mary which shall first happen next before my Decease and shall yearly and every year make up state and adjust in a book to be kept for that purpose a just and true account of the Rents and Profits of the said Farm and Premises called Perry Court so devised to them and their heirs as aforesaid and subscribe their names thereunto and shall afterwards divide the Clear Money annually arising out of the said Estate into Twelve equal parts or proportions and the Inhabitants of Kew Green having ever since ye consecration of the said Chapple in a very commendable manner annually solemnized the twelfth day of May (being the day on which it was consecrated) by resorting thither to hear Divine Service and a Charity Sermon preached before them which good custom is to be hoped will for ever be observed by the said inhabitants. It is my Will that they shall yearly and every year upon the said 12th day of May immediately after Divine Service is ended Distribute and Pay in the said Chapple the said twelve parts or proportions of such clear money so arising out of the said estate in manner following That is to say One clear twelfth part thereof unto the Minister and applied towards the support of a Charity School at Kew Green when such a school shall be there set up and Supported for teaching poor children to Read, write and cast accounts and for instructing and educating them in the Church Catechism and in the Faith and Principles of the same Church; and untill such a school shall be there set up and supported it is my Will that such clear twelfth part of the profits shall be laid up and preserved by the said Minister and Chapple Wardens as a Stock or Fund for binding and placing out Apprentices to handy craft or other trades or to husbandry such child or children of the Poor Inhabitants of Kew aforesaid as are or shall be at any time hereafter Educated or Instructed as aforesaid in any or either of the Charity Schools hereinafter mentioned as my said Trustees and the Survivors or Survivor of them and his or their heirs & assigns shall think fit. But if it shall happen that there are no such Charity Schools set up and supported then it is my Will that the Twelfth part of the said Clear profits as is hereby intended for the benefit of the Poor Children of Kew aforesaid shall be applied by the said Minister and Chapple Wardens . . .

The Charity Schools named as beneficiaries were:

Boys and Girls School at Richmond, Boys Schools at Mortlake, Brentford Butts, Ealing, Chiswick, Hammersmith, Cheltenham and Tewkesbury in Gloucestershire, Faversham in Kent and Haltwhistle in Northumberland. Girls school at St Andrews, Holborn (where Lady Capell was born) in addition to the Charity School at Kew.

There being no Charity School at Kew the income from this trust was retained by the Chapel which was now well endowed:

From pews or seats in the Chapel	£72.0.0.	
less 5 pews which were discharged from paying the Minister's maintenance	12.0.0.	
which reduces the Pews to		60.0.0.
£200 from the Trustees and £200 from Queen Annes Bounty laid out for purchase of lands in Essex (The Woodlands) yearly value of about		20.0.0.
Futher endowment from Dame Holford and Queen Annes Bounty—not laid out		11.0.0.
Lady Capell's bequests about		19.0.0.
From births, burials & marriages uncertain		

a total of probably £120-130.

On February 22nd 1726, the Revd William Comer, M.A. became Vicar of Kingston upon Thames and it was said that he took all the emoluments of Kew Chapel and paid to the Curate only £30 per annum—which led to the lawsuit mentioned later. In about 1729 a sub-Curate was appointed, the Revd Thomas Morell, who assisted the Revd Lewis until the latter ceased to perform his duties in 1733. No curate was appointed at that time and The Revd Morell continued to serve the Chapel. The Revd Morell was born in Eton and educated there, afterwards going to King's College, Cambridge. He was Rector of Buckland in Hertfordshire and chaplain of Portsmouth Garrison. He lived at Turnham Green for many years and was an intimate of Hogarth whom he was said to have assisted in the writing of 'The Analysis of Beauty'. He republished the 'Four plays of Euripides', the 'Prometheus Vinctus' of Aeschylus, a Lexicon of Greek Parody, an Abridgement of Ainsworth's Latin Dictionary and a translation of Seneca's 'Epistles'. He was married in Kew Chapel on April 6th 1738 to Ann, daughter of Henry Barker of the Grove House.

When the Revd Lewis died in 1741 the curacy became officially vacant and the Vicar of Kingston, Wm Comer, sought to take it upon himself and secured a Licence from the Bishop of Winchester. Christopher Appleby, being a lawyer and ever anxious to protect the assets of the Chapel, sought Counsel's Opinion from Mr J. Strange as to how this could be prevented. This is the case he presented:—

The vicarage of Kingston upon Thames in the County of Surrey is very antient, and endowed and has the Chapples of Molesy, Eshaw or Sandy Chapple, Petersham, Richmond & St. Anns Kew Green belonging thereto as chapples of ease to the mother church.

Kew Green is scituated within a parcel of His Majesty's mannor of Richmond and within the parish of Kingston and about five miles distant from it.

26

In the year 1713 the Inhabitants of Kew obtyned a Licence from Queen Ann (with the consent of the then Vicar of Kingston for their own convenience and accommodation and at their own expense) to Erect the last of the abovenamed chapples on Kew Green (part of ye Wast of ye manor of Richmond). Pursuant to this Licence the Chapple of St Anne Kew Green was erected by voluntary contribution and a small endowment of about £5 a year was purchased and settled for keeping it in repair & the surplus above such repairs and the whole till such repairs were wanted to be applyed towards the curates maintenance.

12 May 1714.

The Chapple was consecrated and in the Act of Consecration there is a Proviso that the Inhabitants shall keep the Chapple & comitary in repair & support and maintain a minister at their own expense to officiate and perform Divine Service therein such Minister or Curate to be nominated by the Vicar of Kingston to be licensed by the Bishop so that to all futurity such minister or curate should be no burthen or charge to the vicar or his successors or to any other besides the inhabitants of Kew. And the then Vicar of Kingston accordingly and at the request & recommendation of the then inhabitants named the Revd Mr Thomas Fogg the first curate thereof who was Licensed by the Bishop who by his Decree injoined Mr Fogg constantly to live and reside at Kew & the like method of Recommendation Licencing and residence hath to the great quiet and satisfaction of the inhabitants been used and observed by all succeeding vicars and curate ever since the Chapple was built till now and never did any duty for the vicar nor were ever esteemed as his curates but separate and distinct ministers of Kew and without any burthen or without his expense of a penny so the vicar hath been to satisfaccon suported and maintained at the expense of the Inhabitants. The Governors of the Bounty of Queen Ann for augmenting the revenues of the poor clergy—in order to the more speedy and effectual promoting her then Majesty's gracious intentions and to encourage others to join with them by their rules and orders proposed and offered to any person or persons who would advance £200 or more that they would out of their revenues add thereto £200 and invest the whole in the purchase of Lands and settle the same for a perpetual endowment of any church or chapple which such benefactors (consistent with their rules and orders) should desire to have augmented—By which proposals many Benefactors joined with the Governors which greatly tended to promote the augmenting many poor Living & curacys. 1715. 1.G.1.

An Act of Parliament passed for rendering more effectual her late Majestys most gracious intentions for augmenting the maintenance of the poor clergy.

Preamble.

In the preamble of which act it is among other things recited that her Majestys Bounty was intended for but not only for parsons or vicars who come in by presentation institution & induccon but by donation or were only stipendiary preachers or curates most of which were not corporations nor had legal succession and were therefore incapable of having a Grant of Lands for a perpetual augmentation agreeable to her Majestys intentions —And that in many places it would be in the power of the Impropriator Donor parson or vicar to withdraw the curates allowance.

Or in the case of a chapple the incumbent of the mother church might refuse to employ a curate or to permit a minister duly licenced & nominated to officiate therein and might officiate therein himself and take the benefit of the augmentation and the curates maintenance would thus be sunk.

Enacting Clauses.

It is enacted that all such churches curacys or chapples which should at any time hereafter be augmented by the Governors of the Queen Anns Bounty shall be and are hereby established to be from that time perpetual cures and benefices.

And that the ministers duly nominated and licenced thereto and their successors should be and are established to be a Corporation and to take in perpetual succession in perpetuity to them and their successors such lands and heriditaments as should be granted unto or purchased for them by the Governors of the Bounty or persons contributing with them.

And that the vicar of the mother church whereto any such augmented curacy or chapple doth appertyn & their successors shall be and are hereby utterly excluded from having or receiving directly or indirectly any profit or benefit by such augmentation.

And if such augmented cures remain voyd six months without nomination of a fit person to be licenced such nominations shall lapse to the Bishop etc. etc.

Encouraged by this act of Parliament Mr Appleby and others since deceased offered to pay £200 to the Governors according to their proposals to augment the Chapple of St Ann which was accepted and having added £200 to their revenues an estate of inheritance was purchased with £360 part thereof and afterwards—Feb 28 1716—By bargain and sale inrolled in Chancery as the statute directs & by other conveyances the Governors allotted and conveyed the said estate to Mr Thomas Fogg Curate of this chapple and his successors for a perpetual augmentation thereof.

And the revenues of the chapple being then about £16 per annum the Governors in conjunction with Mr Appleby according to the Lady Holford's will have agreed to augment this chapple which last augmentation money, being £400, is out at interest and with the remainder of the first augmentation is not as yet laid out or invested in a purchase or settled.

1742 May or June.

In the latter end of May or beginning of June last Dr Lewis, the last duly nominated and licenced curate of this chapple dyed.

Since whose death the Reverend Mr Wm Comer the present vicar of Kingston (the mother church) hath (in direct violation and contrary to the Letter and Meaning of the statute of the 1st of King George 1st and to what has hitheto been done by his predecessors ever since this Chapple was built) taken the same into his own hands and will not name a curate to be licenced by the Bishop And has irregularly obtained the Bishops Licence to officiate in this augmented chapple as minister thereof (which licence is irregular being granted by the Bishop after a caveat entered by Mr Appleby without summoning or appointing any time to hear and determine the caveat) which in due time will be disputed and as Mr Appleby is advised recalled and set aside in a propper place.

Whether Mr Appleby may not (tho this is a new case and perhapps the very first of the kind) upon motion obtyn a mandamus out of the court of Kings Bench commanding Mr Comer to nominate a curate to this chapple (besides himself) and what affidavits or evidence is propper on such motion to lay before the court and must the Bishop be a party and appear before the court on this occasion Or what other remedy must Mr Appleby take to obtyne relief in this case and the benefit of this statute.

Mr Strange's opinion.

I am of the opinion that the court of Kings Bench will not grant any such Mandamus as is propsed, the right of nominating being in the nature of a private interest in the Vicar and the default of his exercising that Right being provided against by Gradual Lapses to the Bishop and if the present vicar does not nominate a Preacher in 6 months the application should be made to an ordinary and so higher till there is a proper nomination.

J. Strange
9th Nov 1742.

In view of this opinion no action was taken and Mr Appleby died early in 1744 and was buried on the 14th April. In 1742, the Revd Wm Comer, perhaps altered to the irregularity of the situation, appointed one the Revd Robert Bluett. a friend of his then living in Devonshire, to be nominally curate at Kew. Bluett at once gave to Mr Comer a Power of Attorney to receive for himself all the emoluments attached to the curacy. Neither Comer nor Bluett attended to the duties of the curacy which continued to be performed by Thomas Morell who took his degree of Doctor of Divinity in 1743. He was apparently becoming dissatisfied with the salary he received from Mr Comer and as a result of his complaints the Revd Comer wrote to him as follows:

Reverend Sir,

The Talk I now assign myself is I assure you, a very disagreeable one to me: nor do I conceive how I can have given you any possible occasion to induce you to have obliged me thus by your last behaviour to let you know that I (being well informed that you are discontented with your quarterly salary for your assistance in ye Chapel of St Anns Kew Green and also that you will no longer as you have all along done acknowledge yourself to be employed there by me) you are therefore exhorted to retire to and take care of your own Living in Hertfordshire & because it will also a saving to you: and because I have received authority from Mr Bluett to tell you that allthough he (the said Mr Bluett) did indeed recommend it to me to grant your request of being continued at Kew Chapel & this at whose motion you very well know (my own) yet that nothing of it or any thing also was agreed upon as the company then present very well know, & that he as far as he might appoint a Substitute to Serve and take care of a cure which we both apprehended to be already expressly reserved to me by Act of Parliament had then substituted only me to serve and take care of ye foresaid cure in his absence as far as he may be concerned in the Supply of it: and that You are further to take notice that you are hereby Desired and required to cease your assistance & to quit your present employment at that Chapel of St Anns Kew Green by Lady Day next at farthest if you desire so much time: and that you provide for yourself otherwise by that time or sooner if it shall prove necessary or most convenient for us for that there will then be no further need of you there & that nither will I who have hitherto paid you nor will Mr Bluett pay for your further assistance there beyond such time as aforesaid & I also take this opportunity to assure you that I will, notwithstanding your utterly unnecessary & unprovoked Renunciation of my friendship, persist on all proper occasions to Repeat ye Proofs of it & that I am still & will be

Reverend Sir,

Your Friend & Most Humble Servant
Willm Comer

December the 24th 1745.

P.S. How in the name of reason could you expect an advancd salary when considering ye great dilapidations ye repairs ye land tax the P -s reduction the K -gs pay allmost two years behind hand I might say I know not when the whole revenue will amount to a clear £30 ano.

For the Reverend Doctor Morell at Kew Green.

Dr Morell then ceased to act as curate but he was fond of Kew and continued to attend meetings of the Vestry until 1748.

The absence of a curate led to the following petition: —

Petition to the Bishop of Winchester against Mr Comer for neglect. (No date—probably December 1745)

To the Right Revd Father in God Benjamin
Lord Bishop of Winchester

May it please your Lordship

We the Chappelwarden and Inhabitants of St Anns Kew Green beg leave to lay before your Lorship the following particulars,

Ever since the dismission of Dr Morell from us which was at Midsummer

30

last, we have had no regular service, One Michaelmas day a Child was brought to be Baptized and no Minister came had not Dr Bearcraft been so kind to come from his lodgings to Baptize it, nor was there anyone to attend on General Hamilton's Lady during her Illnes or to give her the Sacrament as she desired but applied to Dr Morell, nor anyone to attend on Mrs Plaistow in her illness who was desirous to have the Sacrament administered to her, had not Dr Bearcraft in his goodness attended her, And since Michaelmas we have had no prayers at all on Weekdays not even on the Saints days or the 5th November, and on the First Sunday of this month if a clergyman had not accidentally been in the Chappel the Holy Sacrament would not have been administered tho we due notice the Sunday before (the person sent being only in Deacons Orders) We therefore humbly petition your Lordship that the Minister who has lived with us 16 years and whome we all esteem, may be restored to us and established among us. We know no offence he ever committed unworthy of his function and we are sure would not wish to be readmitted, but at the General Request of every inhabitant, but we leave it to your Lordship's pleasure to appoint someone or other that may reside & perform regular Service   So

prayeth yr Lordship's
Most Dutifull and
Humble Servants,

Richard Butt	I do realey belive & know those
John Dillman	omissions & neglects to be true
Joseph Noy	in my wifes illness could get no
Thos Lupton	clergyman of this place to pray
John Layton	to her and I toke a papist
James Croome	to Mr Blewit & Mr Comer who
Jos Coleman	beged to be instructed &
John Gater	converted & altho ye man is
Humphry Jenks	here this three months yet
Edw Hobbs	no Just Notice taken or ye
Fra Porter	least paines taken to convert
William Plaistow	him

Arch Hamilton.

This led to the resignation of the Revd Robert Buett in February 1746 and the appointment of the Revd Daniel Bellamy. Bellamy was assistant to the Vicar of Kingston, where he resided, and was later appointed curate of Petersham (June 18th 1747). He appointed the Revd Mr Sampson, who lived at Wandsworth, as assistant curate at Kew.

The Chapel was now in need of repair and funds not being available the Vestry began their investigation of the matter.

At a Vestry held in the Chappel of St Anns Kew Green
after due notice given by the Clerk.
April the 20th 1747.

Memorandum.

Whereas the endowment of the Chappel seems to us to be allotted, by indenture, to the repairs of the said Chappel from Time to Time; and the residue to be given to the Minister; and whereas the late Ministers have appropriated the whole revenue to their own use, we have reason to think that there has been great mismanagement on the said estate; It is agreed

That the Chappel Warden & Overseer inspect the said endowment & that they acquaint the Revd Mr Bellamy Minister with the time of their going; That if he pleases, he may go or send another person on his Part—

Fra Porter, Ed Hobbs, H. Jenks, T. Morell, John Dillman, William Plaistow, John Gater, Richard Butt, John Layton, James Croome, Robt Frime, Joseph Coleman.

The Revd Daniel Bellamy was also at this meeting.

There is no note on the outcome of this inspection. Mr H. Aston, Attorney was then engaged to examine documents regarding the Charity moneys and the Comer affair which he did in November and December 1747 —his fees being £9.17.10, and there is a note, undated. but probably of 1748/1749:

Pulpitts Farm.

50 acres of land at £20 a year in the possession and occupation of Mr William Brannard at his farme in the parrish of Rochford in the County of Essex the rent is paid to Mr Comer at Kingston a years rent is due at Michaelmas but Mr Brannard designed to pay his years rent soon after Christmas to Mr Comer at Kingston.

about 18 acres of Woodland nigh Rochford sold by Mr Comer about 3 or 4 years ago to Mr William Carr & cutt down.

It is clear that, as the result of the examination of documents by the Chapel Warden and the Overseer, the Vestry's suspicions about the 'mismanagement' of the 'Woodlands' estate was confirmed. So they sent two of their members into Essex to see for themselves the condition of the woodlands. William Plaistow had lived in Kew for more than thirty years, had been a regular subscriber to the Chapel and was Chapel Warden in 1731 and 1742. At this time he was about 65 years old. His companion was John Layton who was Overseer of the Poor and who died in 1763. In 1757, in his reply to the interrogatory taken before the trial, Plaistow described the visit thus :

The inhabitants of the said Chapell not then knowing that the said Wm Comer had cut down the woods sent this deponent and one John Layton the overseer into the County of Essex to see in what state and condition such underwood was then in and when they came to the Tenant of the woods and underwoods he told them that by Mr Comer's directions the woods were all cutt down both Great and small and that the Great wood was sold to one Mr Carr and sent to London and that the small stuff was sold for oyster faggots.

Several of the inhabitants of Kew applied to Wm Comer for payment of the money he had received for the trees but without result.

The Vestry, at its meeting on the 11th April 1748, agreed:

That the case concerning the woods etc be laid before Council and likewise how the several books and papers in the hands of Mrs Appleby, relating to this Hamlet, may be recovered from her.

Things moved very slowly and at the Vestry meeting on the 3rd May 1753:

It was agreed by all present that the Minister and Chappel Warden do wait on Mrs Appleby and demand certain Books papers and parchments belonging to the said Hamlet of Kew and now in her custody and in case she refuses to deliver the said books etc to the Minister and Chappel warden it is ordered by the said Vestry that an Attorney be employed to oblige her by due course of Law to deliver the said books papers etc.

The books and papers etc being recovered the lawyers were able to proceed with the preparation of a case and at a meeting on the 29th November 1754 the inhabitants agreed to take legal action against Mr Comer.

The inhabitants were also dissatisfied with the Curate and yet another petition was addressed to the Bishop probably at the instigation of William Frime who became Chapel Warden in April 1754.

To the Right Reverend Father in God
Benjamin Lord Bishop of Winton

The humble Representation of the Inhabitants of Kew Green in the County of Surrey whose Names are hereto subscribed in Behalf of Themselves and the Rest of the Inhabitants there.

MOST HUMBLY SHEWETH

That her late Majesty Queen Ann by Lycence under her Sign Manual date the 28th day of June 1712 granted to the Inhabitants of the Hamlet of Kew Green in the County of Surrey A Peice of Waste Ground with liberty for the said Inhabitants to enclose the same and thereon to erect a Building or Chapel of Ease to the Parish Church of Kingston in the said County which lies remote and at a great Distance from the said Green which said peice of ground was afterwards inclosed and a Chapell erected thereon by the Contribution of the said late Queen and the said Inhabitants which said Chapell was afterwards consecrated and a Fund Raised for the endowment thereof to the Amount of £100 a year and Upwards.

That the Minister or Rector of the said Parish Church of Kingston hath from the Erection or Consecration of the said Chapell always nominated and appointed A Minister to serve the Cure thereof

That Mr Comer the present Rector of Kingston hath appointed the Revd Mr Bellamy the Curate of the said Chapell who lives and resides at Kingston aforesaid which said Mr Bellamy hath appointed under him the Revd Mr Sampson to do the Duty of the said Chapell under him which said Mr. Sampson lives and resides at Wandsworth in the said County greatly distant & remote from the said Chapell

That the said Chapell being so well endowed and having such great Encouragement the Inhabitants of the said Hamlet had great Reason to hope and expect that the said Curate would have constantly resided at Kew Green aforesaid that He might have always been ready to have performed the several parts and offices of his Ministerial Function especially in Cases of Necessity as the Administration of Baptism to Infants in Danger of Death and in Praying with Sick Persons and administering the blessed Sacrament to them in the latest Hours of Extremity in Case of any sudden or dangerous Illness and by Reason of the non Residence aforesaid the said Chapell is neglected and the Duty thereof omitted upon Wednesdays and Fridays as usual to the great Grief and Concern of the said Inhabitants. Therefore the said Inhabitants think it is become a Duty incumbent upon them to lay before your Lordship the several Articles of Complaint following

First—That neither the said Mr Bellamy nor the said Mr Sampson or either of them do not reside upon or near Kew Green by reason whereof the said Inhabitants in Cases of Necessity are destitute of any Assistance from them or either of them and have several times been obliged if they could to get some other Minister to Officiate in their Room and when they have not been able so to do several great Inconveniencys have happened and many more may hereafter happen and especially with respect to the particulars before mentioned

Secondly—The said Mr Bellamy and Mr Sampson have for a long time past neglected and omitted the Performance of Divine Service in the said Chapell on Wednesdays and Fridays whereby the Inhabitants are deprived of attending Divine Worship on those days which they were formerly allowed and permitted to do

Thirdly—The said Mr Bellamy and Mr Sampson or one of Them have for a long time past kept and detained all the money collected at the Sacrament and though often desired by William Frime the Chappell Warden of the said Chapell refuse to distribute the same or any part thereof for the Relief of the poor Inhabitants or to give any Account or let him know to what Pious or Charitable Uses the same is Applyed and although the said Inhabitants have diligently enquired they are not able to discover that He hath given away any of the said money or at least but a very small and inconsiderable part thereof to any of the Poor Inhabitants within the said Curacy

ALL which said Matters are in great Humility represented unto your Lordship by the said Inhabitants who humbly request your Lordship to recall, the Licence you have been pleased to grant to the said Bellamy and Sampson or either of them and to discharge them from further officiating in the said Chapell or at least that your Lordship will please to Oblige the Curate of the said Chapell constantly to live inhabit and really reside at Kew Green aforesaid and to give the said Inhabitants such Relief in the matters hereby represented as may tend to the Glory of God and the Service of his Church as to your Lordship seem meet and necessary.

A copy only of this petition exists and has no signatures. There is no record of any direct result of this petition but Daniel Bellamy continued as curate, became minister of Kew & Petersham when they were consolidated in 1769 and remained so until his death on the 15th February 1788.

The legal investigation proceeded and the initial problem was to decide who was to be proceeded against. The legal ownership of the 'Woodlands' was difficult to establish and so it was decided to include as defendants Wm Comer, who claimed ownership as Vicar of Kingston; George Wilson, the grandson and heir at law of Christopher Appleby who was the last survivor of the original trustees; Samuel Underhill, the legal representative of Jonathan Fogg; Daniel Bellamy, the present nominated curate and Buckland Nutcombe Bluett, the heir of Robert Bluett who was curate at the time the woods were cut down.

In January 1755, William Frime, Chapel Warden, issued the following authority:

I do hereby Authorize and impower you on behalf of myself and the rest of the Inhabitants of the Hamlet of Kew in the Parish of Kingston and the County of Surrey whose Names are sett and Subscribed to a Paper Writing dated Twenty Ninth Day of November 1754 to file a Bill, Information or Plaint in the High Court of Chancery against William Comer Clerk and others as shall be judged necessary and to Proceed therein And for so doing this shall be your sufficient Warrant—
Dated this Twenty Second Day of January One Thousand Seven Hundred and Fifty Five

Wm Frime.

To Mr Thomas Whitfold
at the Chancery Office.

The Information to the Lord Chancellor was filed on the 31st January 1755 and the process began, the Attorney General acting on behalf of the Inhabitants of Kew.

In the course of the investigations prior to the hearing many people were interviewed and from the interrogatories there are some replies throwing light on the condition of the Chapel:

Robert Frime, innkeeper, aged 48 or thereabouts, was brother of Wm Frime, Chapel Warden. and had himself been Chapel Warden in 1745 and Overseer in 1751. He stated that:—

In 1741 the Carpenters Bill for new pales and for altering and repairing the cupula was	£27.13. 0
the Smiths Bill for repairing the cupula and mending the locks and hinges to the gate was	8.16. 0

In 1745 the Carpenters Bill for new paling about
the Chapel was 17. 0. 0
the Glaziers Bill for mending windows 6.11. 0
the Smiths Bill for mending the Pew 1. 6
In 1746 the Bricklayers Bill for mending the Tiling 2. 8. 4
the Plumbers Bill for mending the gutters 1. 3.10½
In 1747 the Carpenters Bill for repairing the
palings and mending the door 18. 2
In 1750 & 1751. the Bricklayers Bill for repairing
the Tiling 1. 5. 6
In 1751 1752 & 1753. the Carpenters Bill for
mending Pales & door 3.11. 8
In 1752 & 1753 the Glaziers Bill for windows 19. 0
In 1755 the Smiths bill for mending the Lock
and Key 5. 6

all at the expense of the inhabitants and not paid for by the Curate.

He further stated that the Chapel was now (1757) out of Repair wanting some new palings and the whole wants new ripping.

Thomas Roberts, surveyor, aged 31 or thereabouts, stated that the Chapel was much out of repair—on the 5th January 1757 he made a survey and by moderate computation it would cost £55.18.0 to put in repair.

The Case against Wm Comer was heard on the 18th and 19th December 1757, the Informants being represented by Mr Robinson and Mr Perrott, their Brief being marked 3 gns and 1 gn.

The Report of the Case is taken from the Decree and Order Book. 1757/8. Public Record Office C33/409 Pt 1. CP 247. (In this transcription, for ease of reading, the abbreviations are extended and punctuations added)

Monday 18/19 Dec.

His Majesty's Attorney General at the relation of Wm. Frime, Chappel Warden of the Chappel of Saint Anne on Kew Green in the Hamlet of Kew in the Parish of Kingston on Thames in the County of Surrey, Thomas Tunstall, John Dillman, Richard Butt, James Orton, James Croome, Henry Mullineux and John Gater, all inhabitants of the said Hamlet, on behalf of themselves and the rest of the inhabitants of the said Hamlet—

Informant—

William Comer, Clerk, George Wilson, Samuel Underhill Esq, Daniel Bellamy, Clerk, & Buckland Nutcombe Bluett Esq,

Defendants—

This cause coming on the 14th day of December and also this present day to be heard and debated before the Right Honorable the Master of the Rolls in the presence of Counsel learned on both sides.

The substance of the Relators Information appeared to be that by Indenture Quadripartite dated the 12th June 1713 between Richard Woolaston Esq of the first part, Benjamin Witton & Oliver Marton Gent of the second part, Joshua Gee & Anna his wife of the third part and John Hungerford Esq. of the fourth part, in consideration of £100 paid by the said J. Hungerford to the said Woolaston and of five shillings apiece to the said Gee, Witton & Marton, the said Gee did bargain, seal and assign unto the said Hungerford, his executors, administrators and assigns the Woods and Woodgrounds, Lands, Tenements & Premises therein particularly mentioned, with the appurtenances, for 500 years, subject to redemption on payment of the said £100 and interest as therein mentioned.

That the said Hamlet of Kew, being a great distance from the Parish Church at Kingston upon Thames, the inhabitants of the said Hamlet could not attend Public Worship at the said Parish Church. Whereupon, about the year 1711, several of the inhabitants by subscription amongst themselves raised a considerable sum of money to be applied towards building a Chappel within the same Hamlet for the benefit of the said inhabitants and the said inhabitants having represented such their design to her late Majesty Queen Ann she contributed thereto and by a Warrant, under her Sign Manual, of the 28th June 1712, granted full License and Authority to the said inhabitants to inclose part of a certain Waste called Kew Green within the said Hamlet, part of the Manor of Richmond, otherwise West Shene, in the said County of Surrey, whereof her said late Majesty was seized in Fee in right of the Crown, and thereon to erect such Chappel.

That afterwards the said ground was inclosed and a chappel erected thereon for the purposes aforesaid out of the said money, which was duly Consecrated and called the Chappel of St Anne on Kew Green in the County of Surrey, and hath ever since been used by the inhabitants of the said Hamlet for the Publick Worship & as a Chappel of Ease to the said Parish Church.

That it being thought necessary to have some provision made for the supporting and keeping the said Chappel in repair for ever and also to make some provision for the maintenance of the curate who should perform Divine Service there, Sir Charles Eyre, Kt., John Lely & Christopher Appleby Esqs., then inhabitants of the said Hamlet and as trustees for all the Inhabitants thereof, did in April 1714 contract with the said Woolaston for the purchase in fee of the several Woods and Wood Grounds in the information mentioned, part of the money so collected and contributed. And thereupon by deed poll indorsed on the said Indenture, dated the 17th Day of April 1714, in consideration of £100 paid to the said Hungerford by Jonathan Fogg, Gent, a Trustee named in that behalf, the said Hungerford assigned to the said Fogg the said Woods and Wood Grounds and other the mortgage, to hold to him the said Fogg, his executors, administrators and assigns for the residue of the said term of 500 years, and it was therein declared that the said Fogg's name was used therein Trust for the said Eyre, Lely and Appleby and that the said term was assigned to the said Fogg to be kept on foot, to go along with the freehold of the said premises the agreed to be conveyed to the said Eyre, Lely and Appleby.

That by indentures of Lease and Release, dated the 16th & 17th April 1714, and by a Fine thereupon levyed, the release being quadrupartite between the said Witton & Marton of the first part, the said Woolaston & Hungerford of the second part, the said Sir Charles Eyre, John Lely and Christopher Appleby of the third part and the said Jonathan Fogg of the fourth part, reciting to the effect aforesaid, in consideration of the said £100 so paid to the said Hungerford, of ten shillings paid to the said Richard Woolaston and of five shillings apiece to the said Witton and Marton, paid by the said Eyre, Lely & Appleby and other considerations, the said Richard Woolaston, Witton and Marton did respectively Grant, Release and Convey unto the said Sir Charles Eyre, Lely & Appleby, their Heirs & Assigns for ever, the Woods & Wood Grounds in the Parishes of Assingdon and Hawkwell otherwise Hockly and South Fambridge in the Hundred of Rochford in the County of Essex and then in the possession of the G. Woolaston, in the information particularly described, with their appurtinences and all their estate and interest therein, to hold to the said Eyre. Lely and Appleby, their heirs and assigns, for ever.

That by deed of bargain or sale, dated the 17th April 1714, duly inrolled, the said Benjamin Whitton, Oliver Marton, Richard Woolastone and John Hungerford, for the same considerations, did also grant and convey the said premises with the appurtinences to the said Sir Charles Eyre, Lely and Appleby, their heirs and assigns for ever.

That by deed poll dated the 30th April 1714 and duly inrolled, the said Sir Charles Eyre, John Lely and Christopher Appleby did declare that the said premises were so conveyed to them in trust, in the first place by the profits thereof to support and keep in repair the said Chappel and until the said Chappel should need or stand in need of such repair, and when the same should from time to time, as occasion should require, be put in good and sufficient repair upon further trust that the said Sir Charles Eyre, Lely and Appleby, or the survivor of them and his heirs, should admit the profits of the said premises, over and above what should be necessary for such repairs, to be received by the curate of the said intended Chappel for the time being towards his support and maintenance so as such curate should diligently and truly perform Divine Service in the said chappel according to the Liturgy and Service of the Church of England.

That the said Jonathan Fogg dyed and the said Defendant, Samuel Underhill is his legal representative as to his personal estate and, as such, is intitled to the legal interest in the said premises for the residue of the said 500 years term, subject to the said trust.

That the said Sir Charles Eyre, John Lely and Christopher Appleby are all dead and the said Appleby was the survivor and dyed about 1744, leaving the defendant George Wilson his grandson and heir at law, who is therefore become seized in fee of the said woods and premises, subject to the said trusts, but he has not hitherto acted therein.

That the Rev. Hugh Lewis, late curate of the said Chappel dyed, whereby the said Curacy became vacant and thereupon the said defendant Comer nominated himself and has ever since acted as Curate of the said Chappel and received and taken the profitts thereof. That the profitts of the said woods and wood grounds depending upon their being cut down at a proper growth and at proper seasons and the said Chappel being out of repair and likely to want a thorough Repair in a few years which would be expensive, the said Appleby, while he was the surviving Trustee, and the inhabitants of the said Hamlett after his death, thought it advisable and to the benefit of the said Charity to let the said woods grow to a proper growth and when the said woods should be of the most value to be cut down, to cut down the same and with the money arising therefrom to make a thorough and effectual repair of the said Chappel; in the meantime to make such repairs, at their own expense, as were absolutely necessary to uphold the said Chappel but reserved the said woods as the only fund for making a thorough and effectual repair thereof.

That the defendant Comer, having by means of taking upon himself the Curacy of the said Chappel got into possession of the said woods and premises, in a private manner caused 25 acres and upwards of the said woods and wood grounds to be cut down, and Sold the wood arising therefrom for £32.8.9d and applyed the money to his own use, being at the rate of £2.5s an acre, whereas the said woods, if they had stood four or five years longer, would have been worth £10. an acre.

That the nomination by the said defendant, Comer, from time to time of a Curate of the said Chappel has been only colourable and the person so nominated hath from time to time been a curate of the said Defendant Comer, attending or serving at some other Church or Chappel of the said defendant Comer and very seldom served or officiated at the said Chappel at Kew Green; but the said defendant Comer procured other persons to perform the cure there and received to his own use the benefit of the curacy thereof, which arise in part from Endowments, Charities or Yearly Stipends, given or appointed by Lady Capell and several other persons for the benefit of the curate of the same Chappel, which amounts to a considerable sum yearly. And insists that he cut down the said woods and sold them by virtue of a Power of Attorney to him for that purpose, given by one Mr Robert Bluett, the then curate of the said chappel, who is since dead, and that he paid to the said Mr Bluett the money received for the said wood so sold, and has his receipt for the same but refuses to produce such Power of Attorney and Receipt.

That the said Robert Bluett dyed many years ago, having made his will and appointed his wife, Jane Bluett, sole executrice thereof, who renounced the executorship; thereupon letters of administration of the personal estate of the said Robert Bluett, with his will annexed, were granted to the defendant, Buckland Nutcombe Bluett, his brother, and by the virtue thereof the said defendant possessed himself of the said Robert Bluett's personal estate, sufficient to pay his debts.

That it was a considerable time before the inhabitants discovered that the said defendant Comer had cut down the said woods, but as soon as they had discovered it, they complained thereof to the said defendant and desired him to pay the money arising therefrom to them and to make satisfaction to the said trust for the damage sustained by cutting down the said wood at an improper growth, that the same might be applyed towards the repairs of the said Chappel, then much out of repair, which if not repaired in a few years will fall down and that the said defendant would deliver the possession of the said woods and premises to the heir of the surviving trustee, or to some of the said inhabitants, for the benefit of the said Trust—but he, under various pretences, refuses so to do.

That the defendant Daniel Bellamy pretends that he is the Curate of the said Chappel, duly nominated, and as such is intitled to all the woods and wood grounds and to cut down and fell the same when he pleases for his own benefit.

That the said defendant Bluett admits the said Robert Bluett was curate of the said Chappel at the time the said woods were cut down and, as such, was intitled to the said woods and to fell and cut the same for his own benefit, but then insists that the said defendant Comer did sell and receive the money for the said woods and applyed the same for his own use, and never did pay or satisfy the same or any part thereof to the said Robert Bluett, but still has the same in his own hands and, therefore, the said defendant, Bluett, as administrator of the said Robert Bluett, ought not to pay the same or any part thereof to the said relators.

Therefore, that the defendants may answer the several matters aforesaid and that the said trust, as to the said woods and wood grounds, may be established and formed; and that the said defendant Comer may account for and pay all the money by him raised as aforesaid by the fall or cutting of the wood off the said woods and wood grounds, with interest from the same, to be applyed towards the repair of the said Chappel, and to make satisfaction for the damages sustained by the said charity and charity estate, by his falling and cutting down the said woods at an improper growth and in an improper manner; and that the defendant, George Wilson, may accept and execute the said trust, now vested in him as aforesaid, or convey the said trust estate to new trustees to be appointed by the Court; and that the said defendant Comer may deliver possession of the said wood grounds and premises to the said defendant, Wilson, or to such new trustees as may be appointed for the said trust estate; and that the said defendants, Comer and Bellamy, may be restrained from cutting down the said woods—is the scope of the relators information.

Whereto the Counsel for the defendant Comer alleges that he, by his answer to the said information, admits the indenture of the 12th June 1713 was executed by the several parties in the information mentioned, that the Hamlet of Kew is within the Parish of Kingston and also within the Chapelry of Richmond about a mile distant, and that the said Parish Church of Kingston is about five miles distant from Kew, and saith that before the erection of the Chappel at Kew the Chappel at Richmond aforesaid was the place of Divine Worship to which the inhabitants of Kew resorted, and to the repairs of which they are by law obliged to contribute and have lately contributed thereto as the defendant believes; and that the inhabitants of Kew, observing that a Chappel there would greatly contribute to the increase of the building and to the better improving of their estates, applyed for leave to erect a Chappel, but they could not obtain their purpose nor would the Bishop consecrate another chappel until they had made some endowment for the maintenance of a curate, exclusive of such dues and rights as were payed and belonged to the Vicar of Kingston and to the Curate of the Chapelry at Richmond, and which dues and rights were accordingly reserved; and that ever since the completion of the said chappel at Kew the curate thereof hath been permitted to enjoy the woods and wood grounds in the information mentioned and fell and sell the underwood thereof for his own use without any demand made by the said inhabitants of any part to be reserved for repairs; . . . and says he believes the curates of the said chappel for the time being, and Dr Lewis by name and his predecessors, proposed the same and cut down all the woods growing hereon, when and as they thought fit, without the consent of any of the trustees and without the interruption of them or any other inhabitants of the said Hamlet, and that the said Dr Lewis dyed in June 1742; admits that soon after his death he procured himself to be licensed as curate of the said chappel by the Bishop of Winchester but, being advised that his said license could not give him any greater power than he had by his institution to the said Vicarage of Kingston, about Christmas 1742, unknown to the said Bluett, appointed him Curate of the said Chappel of Kew and acquainted him by letter, he being then in Devonshire therewith, who accepted thereof merely to serve the defendant for soon after he was licensed and had taken possession of the said curacy, he came to the defendant's house at Kingston and brought with him a draft of a Letter of Attorney and ordered the defendant to inscribe the same, which he accordingly did and afterwards the said Bluett duly executed the same, whereby he appointed him, the defendant, to be his lawful attorney, to receive for his use from the Governors of the Bounty of Queen Anne for the augmentation of the maintenance of the Poor Clergy, or to their Treasurer, or whom else it might concern, all such augmentation money as should from time to time become due to him from the Queen's Bounty as Curate of the said Perpetual Curacy of St Anne's Kew Green, and to give proper receipts and discharges for the same, and also to receive for him and for his use, of and from all person whatsoever whom it might concern, all perquisites and emoluments whatsoever that should from time to time arise and become due to him as Curate for serving the said curacy perpetual of St Anne's Kew Green, and on receipt thereof, to give discharges, if occasion for the same and he did thereby ratify and confirm all and whatsoever his said attorney should lawfully do or cause to be done for him and in his name in and about the premises;

and says the said Bluett lived with him the said defendant at Kingston in that year and afterwards and frequently officiated himself in the said chappel on Sundays and that, during the said Bluett's curacy, he the defendant frequently officiated himself and generally every other Sunday as well as at other times; and that while the said Bluett was at the defendant's house, he, the defendant, found him in lodging, meat, drink and wine, tea and coffee and entertained his company, which was very numerous, and boarded his servant and, as a recompence therefor, the said Bluett permitted him to receive the whole profitts of the curacy, after paying the sub-curate who, with the said Bluett and the defendant, performed the cure during the time the said Bluett was curate;

admits Dr Morell was employed as sub-curate during the greatest part of the time that the said Bluett continued Curate and that Mr Frances and Dr Lillington were sub-curates during the remainder of that time and that the defendant payed them their salaryes by the order of the said Bluett while they respectively officiated and that he, the defendant, received the profitts during the said Bluett's curacy by his order, and while he lived with him the defendant verbally accounted with him for the profitts of the said curacy;

and says the said Bluett resigned the curacy in February 1746/47 and believes the whole time of his curacy, and particularly when the defendant cut the said underwood, the said Chappel was in good repair and that there were no likelihood of its being out of repair for many years and believes, during the whole time aforesaid, the Chappel Wardens for the time being, at the several yearly visitation, made their presentments 'omnia bene' which they would not have done had the Chappel been out of repair and believes that when they made the said presentments they had notice of the falls of the said underwood and during the said Bluett's lifetime neither the Chappel Wardens nor any of the relators found fault with such underwood being cut nor ever called on him, the defendant, or the said Bluett to account for the same;

and believes the said Bluett dyed possessed of a considerable estate and saith the defendant, Bellamy, after Bluett's resignation, was appointed curate of the said Chappel by him the defendant and licensed by the said Bishop;

denys that he has ever acted as Chaplain or Curate of the said chappel otherwise than during the vacancy aforesaid and has not taken any profitts belonging to the said Chapelry save such as belonged to him by law as

42

Vicar of Kingston or in right of the curate to whom he accounted;

admits that, by order of the said Mr Bluett the curate and for his use, he, the defendant, in 1744, 1745 & 1746, cut down some underwood from the said premises, which was sold for £32.8.9. and he the defendant received and accounted for the said money to the said Mr Bluett, the then curate, and believes the said underwoods were cut at a proper growth and sold at its full value, and was informed and believes the same was of a very bad sort and of small value and that they ought to have been cut before to render them the more valuable for the future; and for the better improvement and preservation of the said woods, he, the defendant, fenced and inclosed the same at his own expence with deep and wide ditches, to prevent the cattle from browsing on the same and therefore submits whether the said defendant Bellamy ought now to be deprived of the effects of the depts care of the said woods under pretence that the whole profitts are to be reserved from time to time solely for the repairs of the said chappel;

denys that he caused that, or any other wood, to be cut off the said premises clandestinely or for his own private use or that any of the said inhabitants ever complained to him of the cutting of such wood or desired him to pay the money arising by the sale of it or to make any satisfaction to the said trust estate or otherwise save by the information; and says he believes that the said inhabitants, by the money they raise from rates for repairs and by the compositions for liberty of erecting monuments and making graves in the said chappel, and the burying ground thereto belonging, are more than sufficient to repair the said chappel, exclusive of the said woods, and that the Chappel Wardens and inhabitants have in hand money sufficient to pay for any needfull repair at present; and says he believes the relator, Wm Frime, is now chappel warden and the other relators inhabitants of the said Hamlet,

and saith that he hath been Vicar of Kingston for 20 years or thereabouts and denys that he claims any right to the said woods, but believes the the said profitts thereof belong to, and have from time to time been taken and enjoyed by, the curates of the said Hamlet for the time being and submits to the Court whether the Curate hath not a right to such profitts—

and Counsel for the defendant Bellamy alledges that he by his answer sets forth to the same effect with the answer of the defendant Comer and that in 1764, the defendant Comer, as vicar of Kingston upon Thames nominated him, the defendant, curate of the said Chappel and that he was licensed by the Bishop of Winchester on the 11th day of February, 1746, old style, by virtue thereof he was, and still is, curate of the said chappel and hath officiated as such and has received, or is intitled to receive, the profitts and advantages belonging to the said curacy; and says the defendant Comer never pretended any right or title to the profitts of the said curacy, excepting such as were reserved to him as Vicar of Kingston to his, the defendants, knowledge; admits

43

he is curate of Petersham and also assistant curate to the said defendant Comer at Kingston and since he has been curate at Kew there has been an open account between him and the defendant and the said defendant Comer sometimes receiving part of the profitts of the said curacy for the defendant's use and the defendant sometimes receiving the tythes and dues of Kingston for Comer's use; says he was never in possession of the said woodlands or concerned himself therewith or received any benefit therefrom; admits the said woodlands are by the said deed of trust appropriated in the first place for the repairs to the said chappel and afterwards and until the said chappel shall want repairing, to the maintenance of the curate for the time being & says he disclaims all rights and title to the said woodland.

Counsel for the defendant Samuel Underhill alledged that he by his answer says he believes . . . that Jonanthan Fogg dyed several years ago, having made his will in writing, thereby appointed Daniel Fogg, John Bernard and Nicholas Godshall executors thereof, all of whom renounced the executorship, and that thereupon letters of administration were duly granted to his widow, Catherine Fogg, and saith he, the defendant, afterwards intermarried with the said Catherine Fogg and that she is since dead and letters of adminstration have been duly granted to him, and insists that he is by virtue thereof become intitled to all the said woods and wood grounds for the remainder of the term assigned to the said Jonathan Fogg subject to such trusts as in the information charged, and is ready and willing to act in the said trust in such manner as the Court shall direct, being indemnified therefor.

Counsel for the defendant George Wilson alledges that he, by his answer, saith that he is heir at law to Christopher Appleby, in the information named, and thereby, as he is advised, is become seized in fee of the woods and trees in the bill mentioned, subject to the trusts also therein mentioned, but never acted in the said trusts nor is willing to do so or to permit the relators to make use of his name for obtaining possession of the said premises, but is willing to assign the trust as the Court shall direct, being indemnified. Counsel for the defendant Buckland Nutcombe Bluett alledges that he by his answer says that Robert Bluett, on being appointed such Curate of Kew Chappel as aforesaid, gave the said defendant Comer a power in writing, as he believes, to receive the said profitts of the said curacy to his own use, and the said Robert Bluett very seldom officiated but did not accept thereof for his own benefit but as a nominal person and in trust for the said defendant Comer, and says he believes the said Robert Bluett dyed about the 18th Dec 1749, having made his will dated the first of the same December, and thereof appointed his wife sole executrix, who renounced the executorship and on the 13th March 1749 letters of administration of his personal estate were granted to him, the said defendant, and says he does not claim from the defendant Comer the money for which the said wood was sold, or any part thereof, or any account for the same and disclaims all right thereto.

Whereupon and upon debate of the matter, on hearing an indenture dated the 12th June 1713, an indenture dated the 17th April 1714, an indenture dated the 30th April 1714, articles of agreement dated the 6th February 1744, signed Wm Comer, a receipt dated the 12th May signed Wm Comer for £32.8.9., paper writings marked letter G H J K & L, an extract from the vestry of the Archdeaconry of Surrey marked, the defendant Wm Comer's first and second answers, a paper writing purporting to be a minute of the Vestry beginning with the words 'At a meeting of the inhabitants in the Chapple of St Anne Kew Green 28th July 1745' and ending with the words 'a chapple rate', paper writing marked 1 2 3 & 21, letter of attorney signed Robert Bluett dated 31st Dec 1742, the answer of the defendant, Daniel Bellamy and the proofs taken in this cause read and what was alledged by the Counsel on both sides—

His Honour Doth Order

That the information be dismissed against the defendants Daniel Bellamy and Buckland Nutcombe Bluett, re representative of Robert Bluett, clerk, deceased, and by consent such dismission is to be without costs; and it is ordered and decreed that the Charity in the pleadings mentioned and the trusts created by the deed of the 30th April 1714, be performed and carried into execution; and the defendant George Wilson, the heir of the surviving trustee, declining to act in the trust, it is further ordered that it be referred to Mr Edwards, one of the Masters of this Court, to approve of seven proper trustees, and the said defendant, George Wilson, is to convey the trust estate to such seven new trustees; and at any time when such trustees shall be reduced to three by death, it is ordered that such three surviving trustees be, from time to time, impowered to name four trustees to act in the place and stead of such deceased trustees and to execute proper conveyances so as to vest the trust estate in themselves and such new trustees for the benefit of the said charity according to the trusts created by the deed of the 30th April 1714; and it is further ordered that the defendant, Wm Comer, do pay to such new trustees to be approved by the said Master, the sum of £32.8.9; it is further ordered that the defendant Wm Comer do pay unto the relators their costs in this suit as far as the same relate to the question concerning the said £32.8.9, to be taxed by the said Master but the relators are to pay unto the said defendant George Wilson his costs of this suit, to be taxed by the said Master.

On the 2nd January 1758, the Vestry held a meeting in the Chapel and agreed a list of names to be recommended as Trustees under the order of the Court.

On the 23rd February 1758, Master Edwards issued the following certificate:—

In Pursuance of the Decree made on the hearing of this Cause, bearing the date the 19th Day of December 1757, I have been attended by the Solicitor for the Relators, none attending for the defendants although duely summoned thereto, as by oath made before me appeared, and the said relators having laid before me a proposal whereby they Propose Thomas Tunstal of Kew Green in the County of Surrey Gentleman, John Dilman of the same place Gentleman, Thomas Howlet Warren of the same place Gentleman, William Frime of the same place Coal Factor, Richard Butt of the same place Nursery Man, Robert Frime of the same place Innholder, and James Orton of the same place Gentleman as Proper Persons to be appointed Trustees for the purposes mentioned in the said decree. I have thought fit to allow the said proposal and do approve of the said Thomas Tunstal, John Dilman, Thomas Howlet Warren, William Frime, Richard Butt, Robert Frime and James Orton as proper persons to be trustees for the purposes in the said decree mentioned which I humbly Certify and Submitt to the Judgement of this Honble Court.

In pursuance of the Order of the Court, on the 14th April 1758, Indentures were signed and sealed which reinstated the original Trust and transferred from George Wilson to the newly appointed trustees the Woods and Woodlands which are now described as follows:

All those woods and woodgrounds lying and being in the several Parishes of Assingdon, Hawkewell alais Hockley and South Fambridge some or one of them in the Hundred of Rochford in the County of Essex, One of which is called by the name of Eight Acres, alias Whitthorpe Wood containing by estimation eight acres, be it more or less, abutting to a wood of Edward Hawkers to the West and to another wood of the said Edward Hawkers to the South and to the lands of Robert Bristow Esq on the East and to another wood of the said Edward Hawkers to the North, one other of such three woods is called and known by the name of Eighteen Acres, containing eighteen acres, be it more or less, abutting to the lands of the said Edward Hawkers on the West and abutting to a cartway on the south and abutting to a wood called Rounds Fall on the East and West to a farm called Roundes Fall, and one other of which three woods is called Twelve Acre wood alias Shoulder of Mutton wood, containing by estimation twelve acres, be it more or less, abutting on the West to a wood of Mr Fetherston, on the South abutting to a farm called Smith's, on the East abutting to a highway that leads to a farm called Bechney.

There remained only the matter of the costs to be dealt with and another meeting of the Inhabitants was called and the Minute reads as follows:—

Whereas Mr Roberts has this day agreed to referr his Bills of Fees and Disbursements, by him delivered in to the Inhabitants of the Hamlet of Kew Green in the County of Surrey, for business by him

46

done for the said Hamlet in the Cause Attorney General against Comer Clerk and others, to two Clerks in Court in Chancery, one to be chosen by himself and the other by Mr John Janes, to be by them taxed and settled in such sort and manner as if the said bill was to undergo a strict taxation before one of the Masters of the High Court of Chancery and has likewise agreed to submit to allow such taxation, Now we, the inhabitants, being the major part of the number of such of them as were present at the Vestry on Easter Monday last, provided such two clerks in Court shall agree, Do hereby agree that, on the said Mr Roberts agreeing and submitting as abovementioned to such taxation, to pay unto him, the said Mr Roberts or his order, so much as shall appear to be due to him on the ballance of such Bill after such taxation as above mentioned shall be had and made thereof, such taxation, the two clerks in Court agreeing, shall be final and conclusive. As WITNESS our hands this 30th April 1759.

John Dillman	George Schennerstedt
Richard Butt	Joseph Hillier
Thos Howlett Warren	John Pepper
Wm Prime	James Clewley
Henry Taylor	William Plaistow
Tho Randall	
James Croome	
Robert Frime	I do agree and submit to the
James Orton	above taxations
Jo Gainforth	
Solomon Hillier	Jno Roberts.

The agreed account from Mr Roberts (the Solicitor) for the relators' costs was £252.1.7. This included the defendant George Wilson's costs of £18.15.9, paid by Mr Roberts on the 20th April 1758. Wm Comer's costs were taxed by Master Edwards at £73.4.7. and he had to pay, in addition to the famous £32.8.9., the sum of £5 for the costs of two insufficient answers, so his total bill was £110.13.4. This left the inhabitants with a bill for £141.8.3.

There is a note on the final account—

1759 February 28. Received of Mr. Hobbins, by virtue of a receipt from the Trustees for his first payment for the woods in Essex, he deducting thereout £1.1.0. paid in earnest £53.19.0.

So the inhabitants were left to pay £87.9.3. which they did on the 9th May 1759.

So ends the sorry story of the legal wranglings over the church's financial affairs, and the sadness of it all was summed up by the Revd Daniel Bellamy in a notice he sent in 1769 to the inhabitants of Kew and Petersham:

It might be imagined, that a Chapel, built and indowed in the Memory of many Persons now living, should not be liable so soon to be hurt by legal

Disputes: Yet too true it is, that the whole Amount, for twenty Years past, of certain Lands, vested in Trust for the Repair of the Building, with a Reserve to the Chaplain, has been consumed in a dispute—where the Minister had not the least concern, except in his earnest, though ineffectual endeavour to prevent such contention.

So ends, too, the story of the Chapel at Kew, for in 1769 an Act of Parliament was passed under which the Curacies of Kew and Petersham were detached from the Parish of Kingston and became a Vicarage consolidated. The Chapel was enlarged by the gracious bounty of King George III and Kew Church was opened on 12th August 1770. But that is another story.

The south east view of Kew Parish Church. 1807.　　　　　　C. De Waley
Enlarged in 1770 at the expense of George III to the design of Joshua Kirby, Clerk of the Works to the Royal Household.

(By courtesy of the Richmond Library)